FARMER

FEEDING THE WORLD

CAREERS WITH EARNING POTENTIAL

CAR MECHANIC

CHEF

COSMETOLOGIST

DOG GROOMER

MASSAGE THERAPIST

FARMER

THE ARTS

———

PRESENTING
YOURSELF

CAREERS WITH EARNING POTENTIAL

FARMER
FEEDING THE WORLD

Connor Syrewicz and Andrew Morkes

MASON CREST
PHILADELPHIA
MIAMI

Mason Crest
450 Parkway Drive, Suite D
Broomall, Pennsylvania 19008
(866) MCP-BOOK (toll-free)
www.masoncrest.com

First printing
9 8 7 6 5 4 3 2 1

ISBN (hardback) 978-1-4222-4326-8
ISBN (series) 978-1-4222-4319-0
ISBN (ebook) 978-1-4222-7490-3

Cataloging in Publication Data on file with the publisher.

Developed and Produced by National Highlights, Inc.
Editor: Andrew Gance
Interior and cover design: Jana Rade, impact studios
Interior layout: Tara Raymo, CreativelyTara
Production: Michelle Luke
Proofreader: Abby Jaworski

QR CODES AND LINKS TO THIRD-PARTY CONTENT

TABLE OF CONTENTS

KEY ICONS TO LOOK FOR:

 WORDS TO UNDERSTAND: These words with their easy-to-understand definitions will increase the reader's understanding of the text while building vocabulary skills.

 SIDEBARS: This boxed material within the main text allows readers to build knowledge, gain insights, explore possibilities, and broaden their perspectives by weaving together additional information to provide realistic and holistic perspectives.

 EDUCATIONAL VIDEOS: Readers can view videos by scanning our QR codes, providing them with additional educational content to supplement the text. Examples include news coverage, moments in history, speeches, iconic sports moments, and much more!

 TEXT-DEPENDENT QUESTIONS: These questions send the reader back to the text for more careful attention to the evidence presented there.

 RESEARCH PROJECTS: Readers are pointed toward areas of further inquiry connected to each chapter. Suggestions are provided for projects that encourage deeper research and analysis.

 SERIES GLOSSARY OF KEY TERMS: This back-of-the-book glossary contains terminology used throughout this series. Words found here increase the reader's ability to read and comprehend higher-level books and articles in this field.

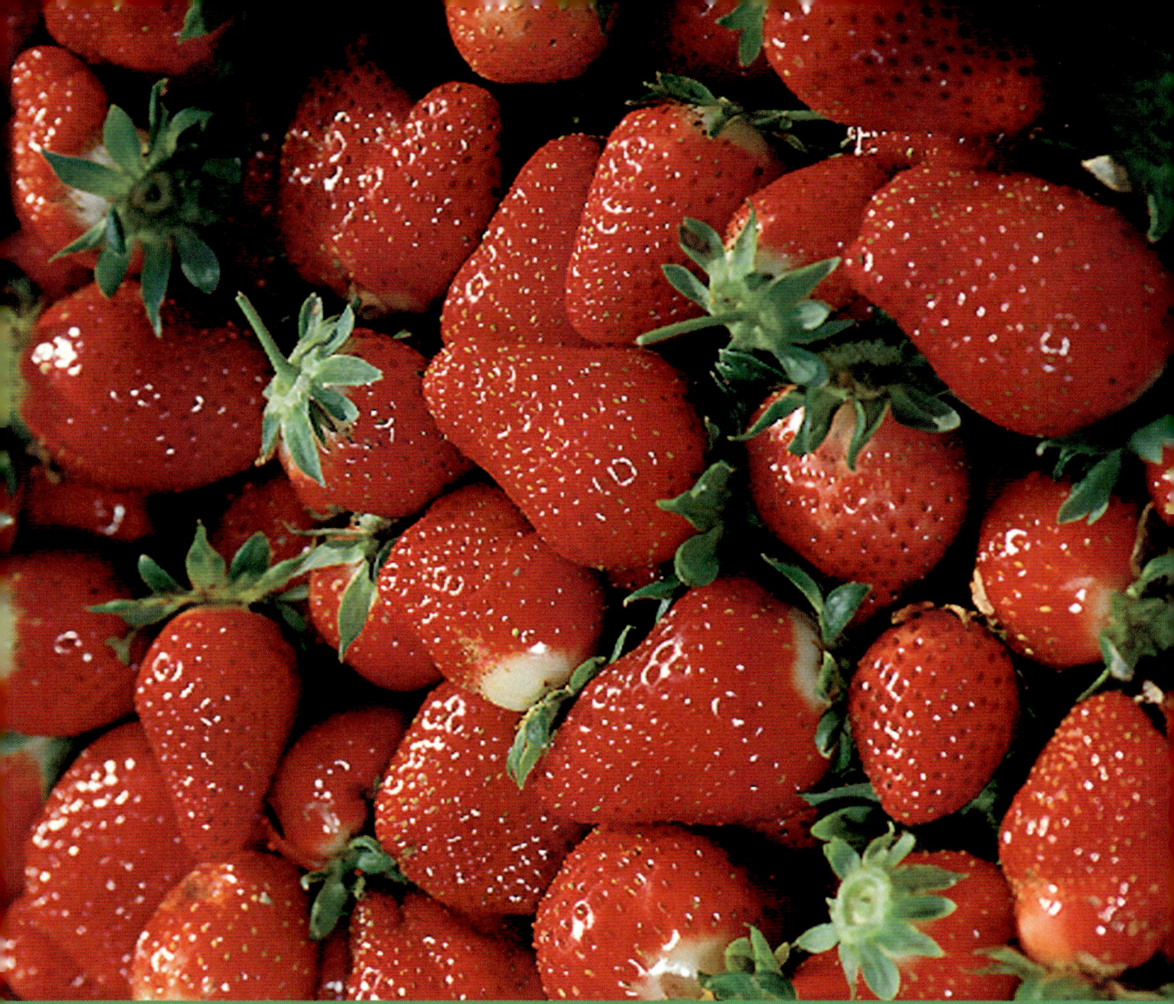

flexible: willing to change one's mind or learn something new

genetics: the study of how living things pass on traits to their offspring

knowledge base: information a person needs to do their job

organic farm: a type of farm that seeks to produce high crop yields without damaging the environment

CHAPTER 1

YOUR FUTURE CAREER

THE ESSENTIAL INGREDIENTS OF LIFE

An abundant food source and a stable supply of water are the two most important ingredients for life on Earth. Many of us, however, do not stop to think about the source of our food.

Food is defined as any substance that is consumed in order to provide our bodies with nutritional support. Almost all food that humans eat comes from plants or animals. However, most people do not raise and harvest crops, nor do they raise any animals besides their pets. Some people have gardens, but very few would know how to produce enough food in their garden to live on if they were no longer able to buy groceries at a supermarket or dine out at a restaurant.

The people responsible for growing the plants and raising the animals that eventually become food and other products work in the agriculture industry. Whether you realize it or not, these men and women have a huge impact on your life!

CAREERS IN AGRICULTURE

The vast majority of the men and women in agriculture today work in careers that do not require a college education. More than half of these people earn on average more than $50,000 a year!

"While this is beginning to change, very few farmers and ranchers are college educated," says James McBride, a former agricultural manager who has owned a farm for only five years—a very short amount of time considering that the average age of farmers in America is fifty-eight. "If you have no experience with farming and ranching," he says, "there are a lot of skills that you will need to learn—and learning these traits today can be difficult. Whether you acquire these skills from experience or from college, there is no agricultural career that does not require hard work and a lot of knowledge."

A *farmer* is someone who grows crops and raises livestock in order to sell these resources as food or "raw materials"—the basic material from which a product is manufactured or made. For example, wheat is harvested and turned into breads, cereals, pasta, crackers, cookies, pretzels, and other products. A *rancher* is very similar to a farmer; however, they exclusively raise grazing livestock, such as cattle or sheep, for meat or wool.

About 80 percent of farmers and ranchers own their own farms, according to the U.S. Department of Labor (USDL). However, on large farms or those that

A farmer cultivates a soybean field in order to control weeds.

are corporately owned, some owners do not participate in all the daily activities required to maintain crops and livestock. The men and women hired to take care of these activities are known as *agricultural managers* and *agricultural laborers* (who are sometimes known as *farmhands*).

As James mentioned, very few jobs in agriculture require a college education, but some do. Examples of such jobs include agricultural engineers and scientists. These kinds of careers, however, account for less than 5 percent of occupations in the agriculture industry, and these professionals are still paid salaries very similar to those earned by farmers, ranchers, and agricultural managers.

THE COLLEGE QUESTION

"More and more farmers and agricultural managers are going to college for agriculture," explains James. For young people who are interested in a farming career, the question of whether or not to go to college has become harder to

U.S. FARM FACTS

- In 2017, the average farm had 444 acres (179.68 hectares), compared to 155 acres (62.73 hectares) in 1935.
- There are approximately 2.1 million farms.
- More than 20 percent of all farmers are classified as beginning farmers—meaning that they have been in business for less than ten years.
- Women make up 31 percent of farm operators.
- The top farm products are cattle and calves, corn, and dairy products.

Source: American Farm Bureau Federation

answer. Agriculture has become increasingly complex. For example, plant and animal breeding today involves complicated sciences such as plant **genetics**—and a wider **knowledge base** is required to remain competitive. "This means that for someone without any experience, acquiring the skills needed for farming today is harder than ever," says James. "Many people do not want to start at the bottom as a farmhand. They see a college degree in agriculture as a way to avoid this."

This is part of the reason that James went to a four-year college to study agriculture, even though he dropped out after his second year. "When I was in high school," he recalls, "I knew I wanted to work in farming but I didn't know the best way to get into the industry." James's mother was a gardener, and she taught him from an early age the importance of being able to grow your own food. "In the summers," he says, "I worked as a farmhand at an **organic farm**. I loved everything about it—working with my hands, tending the animals, and plowing the fields. Seeing the crops grow was one of the best feelings I've ever had."

While a summer job was a great way to begin to learn about the agriculture industry, James decided to go to college for many reasons. "My parents offered to pay my college tuition, so I wouldn't have had too much debt [money that is loaned to someone and that must be paid back] to worry about afterward." Although James was lucky, student debt is an issue that affects many college graduates. The *Wall Street Journal* reports that students who graduated from college with debt had average debt of $37,712. This much debt takes more than ten years to pay off!

"When I was in high school," James says, "a lot of my friends were going to college. I wanted to go too, but for many of the wrong reasons. I wanted the college lifestyle, but I wasn't all that interested in going to classes. Don't get me wrong. I like learning, but education wasn't a priority for me. The kind of learning that I like is being able to see what you are talking about firsthand. There is a big difference between being told how something works in a classroom and seeing something work on a farm. If you pay attention, experience can be one of the best educations you can get."

James is right. No matter what career you want to pursue, firsthand experience in a job can be one of the most important factors for an employer deciding whether or not to hire you. Depending on what career you choose, experience can be more important

A farmer tends his crops.

than a college education. This is part of the reason why, according to CNN, half of all college graduates are either unable to find a job or end up finding a job that doesn't require a college degree!

Not everyone will be lucky enough to have a farm nearby where they can explore this industry firsthand. But James did what any person facing a decision should do—he explored his options. "One of the best things I ever did was take time to learn about the industry. When I made the decision to drop out of college, I didn't feel like there was anything that I was missing. I knew that because of my experience I could get a job—and that with a job, learning all I needed to know would be only a matter of time."

James began his career as a farmhand for a large, family-owned farm in California. While most job candidates need about five years of industry experience in order to be considered for a job in agricultural management, James was promoted to this position after only three years. "I was promoted so quickly," James says, "because I worked hard and learned as much about farming as I could while I was working."

No matter what career you select, success will be difficult if you aren't willing to acquire new skills. Taking the time to explore your interests, passions (something that you care about a lot), and hobbies can lead to a lot of valuable skills. Perhaps the most important skill any young person can develop is learning itself.

"Getting an education can be very difficult," James says, "especially if you are trying to learn something that you do not care for or enjoy. But regardless of your career, there will be certain responsibilities that you do not like but have to do. Learning how to learn means being **flexible**. It means trying your best whether you like what you are doing or not."

Should you go to college? That's an important question. To help find the answer, first respond to these questions: What do I love to do? What are my hobbies? What do I have a passion for? What are my options? Do I have to go to college to get the skills I need to be successful?

Going to college may be your best option. Or another road might lead you to success. Either way, consider every option and be open to all possibilities. And most of all, be willing to learn and work hard, no matter where life takes you!

Getting hands-on experience on a farm during your summer vacation is a great way to determine if a career in agriculture is a good match for your skills and personality.

RESEARCH PROJECT

How do you like to learn? Via hands-on training? In formal classes? Or via a combination of these learning strategies? Write a one-page report that summarizes the pros and cons of each educational method.

TEXT-DEPENDENT QUESTIONS

1. What is the average age of farmers in the United States?
2. What made James want to become a farmer?
3. What is the average college debt?

WORDS TO UNDERSTAND

communal: a type of lifestyle that includes resources that are shared by everyone living in a community

nutrients: substances plants and other living things need to grow and that they cannot make on their own

soil erosion: a naturally occurring process in which topsoil is worn away by the natural physical forces of wind and water

stampede: when a group of animals or human beings runs suddenly in a panic because of a real or perceived threat

tedious: tiring and dull

CHAPTER 2

WHAT DO FARMERS DO?

MODERN FARMING

Farmers and ranchers use plots of land to produce fruits and vegetables, dairy products, and raw materials for other industries. That sounds fairly simple, but modern farming is a complex industry. Not only do farms come in many different sizes, but farms also produce many different products (not just food!). This means that a number of different careers are available to someone who is interested in the agriculture industry.

"Farming" refers to the production of food and other products by growing and raising either crops or livestock. Crops are plants such as fruits and vegetables, while livestock refers to animals such as cattle. While both can be produced on a farm, a ranch is a large area of land that is used only to raise livestock. The term "ranch" has come to refer to any farm that raises any kind of livestock, although traditionally, ranching meant raising those that "graze"—a type of feeding where animals eat widely available plants, such as grass, on large tracts of land.

"There isn't a huge difference between crop production and ranching," says Christian Valencia, who owns a large farm and ranch in Texas, the state with the most ranches in the United States. "Most farms do both. For example, many ranches that end up only selling animal products also grow crops in order to save money feeding their animals, and many farms that only sell crops or produce end up selling their crops to ranches as animal feed." In fact, according to OneGreenPlanet.org, 33 percent of all crops grown in the world are fed to livestock. "Even though so many places do both, the methods used to grow crops," Christian says, "are very different from those used to raise livestock."

During the busy months of the year, more than one hundred people work at Christian's farm. These farmhands are responsible for operating machinery and doing physical labor under the supervision of an agricultural manager.

A farmer harvests corn.

Because agricultural work is only available during particular seasons, farmworkers may only make up to $30,000 a year. Nevertheless, agricultural work can be a great way to learn about the farming industry and get the experience and knowledge needed to be employed in better-paying careers in the industry—or eventually own a farm.

A young dairy farmer discusses why she loves her job.

POPULAR FARMING AND RANCHING CAREERS

There are many career options in agriculture. The following paragraphs provide more information on popular occupations.

Agricultural managers oversee the daily operation of one or more farms, ranches, nurseries (places where trees and plants are grown for sale to the public), vineyards (places where grapes are grown), greenhouses, or other agricultural establishments for corporations and farmers.

Crop farmers grow fruits, vegetables, grains, and other crops. When the crops have finished growing, they harvest and prepare them for shipment to customers.

Livestock, dairy, and poultry farmers and ranchers feed and care for animals in barns, pens, and other farm buildings, as well as on feedlots.

Horticultural specialty farmers supervise the production of vegetables, flowers, and plants (including turf) used for landscaping (modifying the land around homes and businesses to make it more attractive). They also grow grapes, berries, and nuts used in making wine and for other purposes.

Aquaculture farmers, who are sometimes known as *aquaculturists*, raise fish and shellfish in water-based systems (cages and pens, inshore and offshore), land-based systems (rain-fed ponds, tanks and raceways, and irrigated or flow-through systems), or recycling systems. They stock, feed, and otherwise care for aquatic life used for food and for recreational fishing.

An aquaculturist harvests tilapia.

CROP PRODUCTION

The types of crops most commonly grown in the United States are corn, soybeans, hay, wheat, and cotton. In other countries, different crops are popular. For example, potatoes, wheat, barley, cabbages, and sugar beets are the most common crops in Germany. "Producing crops," Christian says, "involves three main stages: preparation and planting, care and cultivation, and harvesting and storage." Depending on the climate, these three stages can take anywhere from eight to eleven months to complete, although depending on the crop that one grows, the phases can often overlap.

During the preparation and planting phase, soil is cultivated and prepared for planting. Preparation usually involves some form of tillage—breaking up hard soil to help plant roots grow more easily and quickly. Tilling a field requires a tool known as a plow. Up until the twentieth century, tillage involved an ox or a horse pulling a plow, but since the early 1900s, tractors pull most farmers' plows.

"The best time to till a field," Christian says, "is right before planting in order to prevent **soil erosion**." This is one of the main environmental concerns related to soil preparation. Since most farms and ranches are located on wide and usually flat land, breaking up and loosening soil means that it can be very easily moved by the wind. The layer of soil that is most quickly eroded is known as topsoil. This soil is **nutrient** rich and very important for the success of a crop.

In the Northern Hemisphere, most crops are planted during the spring and late summer months, between the beginning of April and the end of June. In the Southern Hemisphere, the majority of crops are planted from September through February (spring and summer in that hemisphere). In today's era of mechanized farming, two large pieces of equipment are used to plant, depending on what kind of seed a farmer is planting. Drills open a small hole in the soil and drop a controlled amount of seed into the hole. Planters open a seed trench, drop seeds into the seed trench one at a time, and gently cover the seed with soil.

"The cultivation phase," Christian continues, "involves caring for the plants once they have been planted. This means managing the nutrients that are available to the plants, controlling pests such as weeds and insects that can harm crop growth, and watering the plants as they grow."

Plant nutrients and pests are, in most cases, managed by the application (spreading) of chemicals. Fertilizers, including manure (a combination of animal feces and straw or other litter), are spread over the farmland to replace nutrients in the soil used up by growing plants. When applied in proper quantities and at appropriate times, fertilizer can significantly increase the amount of a crop

COMMON AGRICULTURE PESTS

Forty percent of global crops are lost to agricultural pests each year, according to ModernAg.org. Insects cause a considerable amount of this damage. Here are some typical agricultural pests:

A Colorado potato beetle.

Locusts can eat their weight in a day and can gather into huge swarms that are up to 460 square miles (1,191.39 square kilometers) in size!

Japanese beetles feed on approximately 300 species of plants and can cause major damage to crops.

Stinkbugs feed on the stems and leaves of plants and the juices of fruits and vegetables such as berries, peppers, beans, apples, peaches, pecans, sorghum, and cotton.

Aphids suck the sap from plants and weaken them.

Corn rootworms, which feed on corn silk and leaves, are increasingly resistant to pesticides. They can be a persistent pest because they also lay their eggs throughout the crop. These eggs fall into the soil and hatch during the next year's corn growing cycle.

Colorado potato beetles, which are resistant to insecticides, feed on potato crops, tomatoes, and eggplants.

Caterpillars are super-fast munchers that can destroy a plant in no time.

Whiteflies suck the sap from plants, weakening them.

Thrips suck the chlorophyll from plant leaves, gradually killing the plant.

Sources: Ledford's Pest Control, Planet Natural Research Center

harvested at the end of the season. Pests are controlled using pesticides, chemicals that are specially designed to kill insects, weeds, and mold, as well as other pests.

A tool known as a sprayer is used to spread these chemicals. The sprayer is either pulled by or mounted on a tractor. This tool may also be

An animal caretaker (left) and an entomologist inspect a cow for fever ticks.

used to water the crops as they grow. However, most farms have very complex pipe systems, known as irrigation, to move water through fields quickly and easily.

"Once all of these phases have been completed," Christian says, "the last stage of the process is to harvest the crops from the fields so that some of them can be sold and others can be stored for the months ahead." According to Christian, the types of tools used to harvest vary from crop to crop. Field crops are harvested by machine, while fruits and other small crops are typically picked by hand.

LIVESTOCK PRODUCTION

A ranch is a large facility dedicated to the production of livestock for milk, fiber (wool, etc.), or meat. A single individual or a family typically owns a ranch, which is usually supported by a large staff that may include family members who work on the ranch. Some large ranches are owned by corporations.

FEWER FARMERS, MORE FOOD

At one time, most of the world's population were farmers. In 1790, about 90 percent of the entire American population, for example, were involved directly or indirectly in agriculture. Given new technology, however, and more efficient farming practices, this number quickly changed.

By 1940, only 18 percent of the American population were needed to grow all of the food the country required. The average farmer then grew enough food for nineteen other people besides themselves—enough that America could start selling its excess food to other countries!

Today, only 2 percent of the American population is involved directly or indirectly in agriculture. The American Farm Bureau Federation reports that the average American farmer grows enough food to feed 165 people!

The process of producing, or raising, livestock is similar to that of growing crops: breeding the animals, caring for them as they grow, and either slaughtering (killing) the animals for meat or collecting products—milk, eggs, or wool, for example—that the animals produce.

"Breeding livestock," Christian says, "means making the animals have offspring." In other words, they give birth to new livestock. A rancher decides which animals to raise—chickens, cattle, or sheep, for example—and then makes decisions about which animals to breed. "A rancher," Christian continues, "must be able to tell which animals are superior and which will produce the best offspring." Doing this requires knowledge about breeding practices and, in certain cases, genetics—a branch of science that studies how specific traits are passed from parent to offspring. In addition to breeding stock, a rancher can also buy stock. Some ranchers focus on buying young stock and raising it.

Once livestock have been born, they must be cared for. "Caring for animals can be very difficult," Christian explains. "You have to know a lot about the ordinary growth of the animals themselves, how much and what kinds of feed to give the young animals, and how to house them."

Certain kinds of livestock, such as cattle and sheep, feed by grazing on grasses, which requires a large amount of land. Allowing animals to graze involves herding (moving) the animals out of housing units—large buildings that protect the animals from weather and cold—and onto the ranchland. Once the animals are on the ranchland, they are allowed to feed freely. However, even this phase must be monitored by a rancher to make sure the animals do not overgraze, which can result in soil erosion. They also need to be monitored so that they are safe from attacks by wild animals such as coyotes, wolves, and mountain lions—although studies show that illness and bad weather are the major killers of livestock.

A poultry farmer tends her flock.

THE MOST DANGEROUS OCCUPATIONS IN AMERICA

Not every worker spends their day in a comfortable office. In fact, some careers can be very dangerous, with workers risking injury and even death as they perform their duties. Careers in agriculture often rank among the most dangerous jobs in the United States. In 2017, the following occupations had the most fatalities (deaths):

1. Fishers and related fishing workers
2. Logging workers
3. Aircraft pilots and flight engineers
4. Roofers
5. Refuse and recyclable materials collectors
6. Structural iron and steel workers
7. Truckers and drivers/sales workers
8. Farmers, ranchers, and other agricultural managers
9. Front-line supervisors of landscapers, lawn service, and groundskeepers
10. Electrical power-line installers and repairers

Source: USDL

Many ranchers grow hay and grain on their ranches to support their livestock's nutritional needs and to avoid buying feed during the winter months when grazing can be very difficult, if not impossible. The rancher is also involved in the herd's health, keeping animals healthy and seeking veterinary care when it is appropriate.

Once the animals have grown into adults, cows are milked, chickens' eggs are collected, sheep's wool is sheared, and some of the animals are slaughtered in order to produce meat. "Some ranchers slaughter their own animals," Christian says, "and sell the meat themselves in order to make more money per animal. But this can be a very complicated process and involves a large investment of money to buy all of the necessary equipment. Most ranchers sell the animals to a slaughterhouse in order to avoid this process."

ORGANIC FARMING AND RANCHING

According to the Ontario (Canada) Ministry of Agriculture, Food and Rural Affairs, "the principal goal of organic production is to develop enterprises that are sustainable and harmonious with the environment." Sustainable means something that can be done without depleting natural resources. In terms of the environment, harmonious means working with the environment rather than against it.

Organic farming and ranching have become popular for several reasons. Many farmers and ranchers are switching to organic production methods because they want to have a more positive interaction with the environment, they believe it creates a safer food supply (by reducing or eliminating the use of chemical fertilizers and pesticides), and the public has expressed a strong desire to eat crops and meat that have been grown and raised in a more environmentally friendly manner. Farmers and ranchers are also going organic because this method is more lucrative (producing more profit)

A farm laborer harvests crops on an organic farm.

than traditional methods. The U.S. Department of Agriculture's Economic Research Service reports that "organic crops can fetch a price premium of anywhere from 25 percent to 200 percent or more over conventionally grown products."

According to the Department, some major components of organic farming and ranching include the following:

- The use of cover crops, green manures, animal manures, and crop rotations to fertilize the soil, maximize biological activity, and maintain long-term soil health
- The use of biological control, crop rotations, and other techniques to manage weeds, insects, and diseases
- An emphasis on biodiversity of the agricultural system and the surrounding environment
- The use of rotational grazing and mixed-forage pastures for livestock operations and alternative health care for animal well-being
- The reduction of external and off-farm inputs and elimination of synthetic pesticides and fertilizers and other materials, such as hormones and antibiotics
- A focus on renewable resources, soil and water conservation, and management practices that restore, maintain, and enhance ecological balance

OTHER CAREERS IN AGRICULTURE

Some farmers decide they want to pursue other opportunities in agriculture. Others choose to work as both farmers and in other agricultural careers. Here are some careers to investigate:

Agronomists use their knowledge of crop and soil science and ecology to improve crop yields.

Crop advisors are agricultural experts. They provide advice on everything from the types of seed and fertilizer to use to pest management and disease treatment strategies to new technologies.

Crop scouts inspect farm fields to identify the presence of animal and insect pests, weeds, and disease, or other animals or conditions that will negatively affect crop yields.

Agricultural pilots fly small planes at low altitudes to apply fertilizers, pesticides, and fungicides on farm fields.

Crop adjusters work in the insurance industry and are experts in both farm finance and agriculture. When farm products are damaged or destroyed by bad weather, insects, disease, or other things, farmers often make an insurance claim to see if they can be reimbursed (paid) for their losses. Crop adjusters inspect fields for which an insurance claim has been made. They decide how much money, if any, will be awarded to the farmer for their loss.

OTHER AGRICULTURAL PRODUCTS

While agriculture is thought of mainly as the industry that produces our food, the raw materials for many other things come from plant and animal products that are grown by the agriculture industry.

Crops that are grown in the United States, for example, are present in many products such as biofuel, a kind of car and truck fuel made mostly from corn products; penicillin, a very common kind of antibiotic medication; alcoholic beverages; and glue.

Livestock, on the other hand, are used to make products such as glue; shampoo; instrument strings; makeup; medicine; fabric softener; linoleum, a kind of tile floor covering; and explosives!

Agriculture science teachers educate high school and college students about farming. In addition to teaching agriculture classes, they also may teach courses in biology, earth science, chemistry, and environmental science.

IS AGRICULTURE RIGHT FOR ME?

"Not everyone is cut out to work in agriculture," says Chris Peterson, a crop manager for nearly twenty-three years. "Being a farmer is really more of a lifestyle than a career. During certain months, you start work when the sun rises and finish when it sets. Most farmers live on the farm where they work, and some people don't like the lifestyle. It's pretty **communal**."

Farmwork can be extremely rewarding, but it also can be **tedious**, exhausting, and frustrating. It's hard physical work, and in some cases, it can even be dangerous. Crop production involves operating heavy machinery, and if you work on a large farm, the machinery can be massive. Operating that kind of machinery has risks. According to Chris, ranchers have it the worst. Trying to move a herd of hundreds of cattle can be difficult, and if the animals get scared for any reason, they can **stampede**. Some people couldn't be paid enough to do that kind of work!

Chris says, "Young people interested in agriculture need to ask themselves if working in agriculture is right for them. A great way to answer this question is by examining your strengths."

He continues, "When I was a kid, I dreamed of the open range, riding horses, the smell of soil, growing tomatoes as big as your head. I really thought that agriculture would be the life of a cowboy. The truth is that you need to be very patient. You need to constantly compromise with factors such as weather and disease that are outside your control, and you have to refuse to get frustrated if you have a bad season. You need to be willing to work with very powerful chemicals. Don't get me wrong—I love the lifestyle of a farmer, but I have the personality for it. I got lucky. If I were to go back and do it all over again, I wouldn't change a thing. But I know a lot of people who want to get into this industry and haven't considered all the things they will need to do. They think it looks pretty from the outside—but they don't know what it's like to live the life on the inside."

An agricultural pilot applies a low-insecticide bait that is targeted against western corn rootworms feeding on and laying eggs in these soybeans.

RESEARCH PROJECT

Learn more about animal and insect pests that damage and destroy crops or affect the health of livestock. What strategies do farmers and ranchers use to fight these threats? Write a 250-word report that summarizes your findings.

TEXT-DEPENDENT QUESTIONS

1. What is the difference between a farmer and a rancher?
2. What is aquaculture?
3. What is soil erosion?

CHAPTER 3

TERMS OF THE TRADE

agronomy: An agricultural specialty that focuses on the use of crop and soil science and ecology to improve crop yields.

annual: A plant that completes its life cycle in one year or less.

aquaculture: The process of growing, under controlled conditions, freshwater and saltwater plants, animals, and other organisms. Also known as **aquafarming**.

arboretum: A botanic garden that is devoted to the display and study of trees and shrubs.

bale: A bundle of cotton, paper, hay, or other product that is tightly wrapped and bound with hoops or cords in preparation for storage or sale.

baler: A farm machine that collects cut and raked straw and hay, and compresses and binds them into bales in cylindrical or square shapes.

botanic garden: A facility where a wide variety of plants and trees are grown and displayed for public viewing and study by plant scientists. Also known as a **botanical garden**.

breed: The looks and characteristics of an animal that make it part of a unique group. Aberdeen Angus, Hereford, Gelbvieh, and Maine Anjou are examples of cattle breeds.

breeding: Controlling how animals mate to create a desired outcome.

calf: A young animal of the bovine species.

cash crop: Any crop that is sold to make ready money, rather than one that is eaten by the farmer or fed to cattle. Examples of cash crops include wheat, corn, potatoes, cherries, apples, soybeans, bananas, cocoa, coffee, sugarcane, cotton, and oranges.

cattle: Domesticated, plant-eating farm animals from the bovine species that are raised for their meat, milk, or hides, or to perform work.

certified seed: Seed that meets the standards of a certifying agency (usually a state government agency). Certified seed is genetically pure and has met a minimum level of quality and other criteria.

combine: A large agricultural machine that harvests grain and threshes it in the process.

compost: A combination of decayed organic matter, soil, and sometimes mineral fertilizers that have been collected, moistened, and allowed to undergo biological decomposition (rotting or decay).

corporate farm: One that is operated by a corporation; these farms typically are very large.

cover crop: A plant that is used to slow erosion, enhance the availability of water, improve soil health, reduce the growth of weeds, help control pests, and otherwise improve agricultural conditions. Cover crops include legumes (peas, beans, red clover, crimson clover, etc.), cereals (wheat, barley, rye, oats, forage grasses, buckwheat, etc.), and other plants.

crop rotation: The cultivation of different crops in a specified order on the same fields in order to avoid depleting (using up) nutrients in the soil, reduce the presence of agricultural pests, and otherwise improve the productivity of a farm.

cultivation: Breaking up and otherwise preparing the land to be planted.

cultivator: A type of large farm equipment that is used to prepare the soil for planting, including removing weeds.

domesticated animals: Those tamed by humans and kept as pets; used to perform labor; raised to provide milk, wool, or other products; raised to eventually be slaughtered for their meat or other products; or utilized for other purposes.

drought: A prolonged period of little or no rain that creates a shortage of water.

dry farming: The practice of relying solely on rainfall and moisture stored in the soil, rather than irrigation, to produce crops.

family farm: One that is operated by one or more members of a family.

farmers' market: A public place such as a park where farmers go to sell their crops and other products to the public.

fertilizer spreader: Machinery that is attached to a tractor and used to spread fertilizer or manure over a field.

fertilizers: Natural or chemical substances that are added to the soil to help make plants grow better.

genetically modified crops (GMCs): Those that have been genetically altered by scientists so that they have higher nutritional value; improved yields; increased resistance to frost, drought, or insect pests; longer shelf life; and other benefits. Debate continues about the safety of GMCs and genetically modified animals.

genetics: A branch of science that studies how specific traits are passed from parent to offspring.

germination: The resumption of the growth of a seed after a dormant period. Soil temperature and the presence of oxygen and water are required to cause a seed to germinate, or sprout.

Global Positioning System (GPS): A satellite-based navigation system established by the U.S. Department of Defense that is made up of at least twenty-four satellites.

greenhouse: A climate-controlled glass building that is used to grow plants during cold weather.

harrow: A type of agricultural equipment that is pulled behind a tractor or all-terrain vehicle to level (flatten) the soil surface, break up manure, redistribute crop residue, and break up weeds.

harvesting: The process of collecting ripe fruits and vegetables from farm fields in preparation for sale to consumers or food companies.

herb: A plant with seeds, leaves, or flowers that is used to flavor food or for medicine or perfume; examples include thyme, rosemary, and mint.

herbicide: A type of pesticide that is used to kill unwanted plants without damaging crops or other wanted plants.

herbivore: An animal that only eats plants or plant-based feedstock.

hydroponic gardening: The process of growing crops in a water-based system rather than in the soil.

infestation: An invasion of insects, parasites, or other unwanted living things.

irrigation system: A mechanical system that supplies water to crops.

livestock: Any domestic animal—including beef and dairy cattle, goats, hogs, sheep, and horses—that is raised to provide meat or other animal by-products (wool, milk, etc.) or to perform work on a farm.

manure: A combination of animal feces and straw or other litter.

nursery: A place where trees and plants are grown for sale to the public.

nutrients: Chemical elements and compounds that promote growth and sustain life.

omnivore: Animals that eat both plant- and animal-origin feeds.

organic farming: A form of agriculture that seeks to produce high crop yields without damaging the environment.

parasite: An organism that lives on or inside another organism to obtain nutrients from it. Flies, ticks, lice, mites, roundworms, tapeworms, and flukes are examples of parasites.

perennial: A plant that lives for many years. They are typically slower growing than annuals, and can live from three to more than seventy years.

pest management: The process of using chemicals, traps, and other methods to control pests such as insects, rodents, and birds that eat and otherwise damage crops.

pesticide: Any substance or mixture of substances that is used to prevent, destroy, repel, or reduce the presence of a pest (insects, weeds, mold, etc.). In large amounts, pesticides can be harmful to both humans and the environment.

plant genetics: Studying and working with the genes of plants to make healthier plants or those that are larger or that offer more fruits and vegetables.

planter: A type of large farm machinery that is used to plant row crops. The farmer directs the planter to open a seed trench, meter seeds one at a time, drop seeds into the seed trench, and cover the seeds with soil.

plow: A type of large farm machine that is used to break up the soil, bring nutrients to the surface, and otherwise prepare the ground for planting.

poultry: Chickens, turkeys, geese, ducks, and other fowl that are raised for the production of meat or eggs.

reaping: The process of cutting grain for harvest.

regenerative agriculture: A type of organic farming in which farmers use agriculture to improve degraded land.

robot: A self-controlled machine that is designed to perform tasks more efficiently and less expensively than can be done by humans. The machines are usually equipped with appendages that allow them to move and interact with their environment. The word "robot" comes from the Czech word "robota," which means "forced work."

robot farming: Agricultural tasks—planting, weeding, harvesting, etc.—that are done by robots.

seed drill: A tractor-drawn farming implement that is used to sow (plant) seed at a precise depth and spacing between plantings over a large area.

seeding: The process of adding seeds to the earth or water (hydroponic gardening) to produce plants or vegetables.

slaughterhouse: A place where animals are killed humanely (quickly and with little or no pain). Unfortunately, animals are not always killed humanely at every slaughterhouse.

soil erosion: A naturally occurring process in which topsoil is worn away by the physical forces of wind and water.

soil nutrients: Those that provide energy to plants for growth. The three main nutrients are nitrogen, phosphorus, and potassium. Other important nutrients are calcium, sulfur, and magnesium.

sprayers: Handheld, backpack-carried, walk-behind, or tractor- or ATV-mounted and -operated devices that are used to apply pesticides.

sustainable agriculture: Farming practices that seek to protect and preserve the environment for future use by farmers. Sustainable agriculture aims to promote a healthy environment while still achieving economic profitability and social and economic equity (fairness).

threshing: The process of separating grain from the plant during a harvest.

tillage: The preparation of soil for planting.

topsoil: The uppermost layer of soil that typically is the richest in organic matter and microorganisms that help crops grow.

viticulture: The science and practice of growing grapes.

weeding: The process of removing plants (known generally as weeds) that are harmful to fruits, vegetables, and other plants grown by farmers.

yield: The final amount of an agricultural or industrial product after harvest or production is completed.

WORDS TO UNDERSTAND

administrative: having to do with how a business or other organization is run

aspiring: trying to reach a goal

private college: an independent school that sets its own rules and policies; these schools are typically smaller, but cost more to attend, than public schools

public university: a school that is funded by public tax dollars and is operated by appointed boards and trustees

CHAPTER 4

PREPARING FOR THE FIELD AND MAKING A LIVING

BECOMING A FARMER

Young people who want to become farmers have several training options. They can go to a vocational school, participate in an apprenticeship, earn a college degree, or teach themselves. All these paths can lead to successful careers in agriculture as long as you're willing to work hard and stick with your dreams.

HIGH SCHOOL

Some high schools offer courses in machine work, and others even specialize in agriculture. At these schools, you can begin to learn practical skills while taking classes toward earning your high school diploma. Agricultural-focused high schools are sometimes even located in or near cities. For example, in the United States, the Chicago High School for Agricultural Sciences offers the following classes:

- Intro to Agricultural Science
- Ag Careers & Leadership
- Civics/Agricultural History
- Agricultural Career Paths
- Environmental Science

If you plan to run your own farm, you'll also need strong math skills, so you should take algebra, geometry, advanced algebra and/or trigonometry, and precalculus.

Farmers are not just good at growing plants and raising animals. They also are skilled businesspeople. To build these skills, take classes in business management, marketing, communications, accounting, and computer science.

Taking foreign language classes will also come in handy because many of the people you work with or manage will come from other countries.

TECHNICAL SCHOOL

Attending a technical school, also known as a vocational school or technical community college, is a great alternative to a four-year college for people interested in becoming farmers or agricultural managers. Such schools offer training in a specific set of skills for a specific industry. Technical schools provide much shorter training programs—generally between six months and two years, depending on what kind of skills you are learning—than four-year schools.

If you study agriculture at a technical college, you'll take classes such as these:

- Introduction to Sustainable Agriculture
- Introduction to Animal Science
- Basic Farm Maintenance
- Field Crop Production
- Soil and Water Management
- Pest Management
- Introduction to Agriculture Economics
- Introduction to Agriculture Marketing
- Applied Agriculture Calculations
- Plant Form and Function
- Introduction to Environmental and Natural Resources
- Introduction to Horticulture

As the agricultural industry becomes more competitive, it's a good idea to consider earning a technical degree to expand your skill set and learn about cutting-edge farming techniques. Tuition at technical colleges is usually significantly lower than at four-year colleges and universities.

A community college student conducts experiments on seeds.

APPRENTICESHIPS AND INTERNSHIPS

"It'll be hard to get hired as anything but a seasonal worker," Chris Peterson says, "if you don't have any experience working on a farm. If you didn't grow up on a farm, and you don't have farmers in your family, the best way to get experience is to apply for an apprenticeship." Apprentices usually have very little prior experience but are hired by a farm in order to be taught while they work. Agricultural apprenticeships usually last for one growing season and sometimes also involve taking classes at a local community college. Apprentices sometimes receive pay, and most receive free housing. As an apprentice, you'll learn how to do the following:

- Crop mapping, planning, and rotation
- Soil preparation
- Seeding
- Transplanting
- Weeding
- Harvesting
- Product washing and packing
- Pest management
- Livestock care
- Farm machinery operation and maintenance
- Compost management

Visit www.beginningfarmers.org/apprenticeship to view listings for apprenticeship opportunities. Reviewing these listings can give you a good idea of what an apprenticeship involves, including necessary skills and typical work environments. Another good source is https://attra.ncat.org/internships.

Learn more about agricultural apprenticeships.

Aspiring farmers can also participate in internships at farms. Internships are paid or unpaid learning opportunities in which a student works at a business to obtain experience. In the agriculture industry, they can last anywhere from a few weeks to a full growing season. They are often a requirement of a two- or four-year degree program, but some farms offer internships to anyone who is interested in pursuing a career in agriculture.

FOUR-YEAR COLLEGE

Earning a four-year degree is not necessary to become a farmer, but people may choose to earn a bachelor's degree for the following reasons:

- They are either aspiring or current farmers who want to gain specialized knowledge by earning a degree in sustainable agriculture, organic farming, agribusiness, plant breeding, agricultural communications, dairy science, or agronomy.

- They are aspiring farmers who don't come from a farming family and are unable to obtain experience or training through other methods.
- They simply want to "grow" their knowledge by earning a four-year degree.

Degrees in agriculture or related fields are typically available at large **public universities**, although they are also offered by **private colleges**.

HANDS-ON LEARNING

Getting a job on a farm can be easy, especially during the busy season. According to Chris, at the end of the growing season and during harvests, farmers usually need all the help they can get. While this kind of work doesn't pay very well and is only seasonal, it can be one of the best ways to break into agriculture. A farmer will notice a hard worker, and if you work hard enough, they may ask you to stay for the rest of the year. Even if they don't, a few seasons of experience on a farm should be enough to enable you to start applying for jobs as an agricultural or crop manager.

All it takes is the willingness to work hard—and get your hands dirty!

HIGH-LEVEL EARNINGS

Many full-time positions in the farming industry pay very well. "But if you want to make really good money, you need to own a farm," explains Angela Stevens, an agricultural manager who has worked on her family's farm for her entire life.

Of all the careers in the agriculture industry, farm owners make the most money on average, but they also take the biggest risks. Most other agricultural workers earn a yearly salary, which they can be sure won't change very much.

Men and women in these careers know they will be paid a fair salary for the work they do every day. If a farm owner cannot pay employees for their time, then a farm goes out of business, and those workers will be eligible for unemployment benefits (cash benefits that are provided by the government for a certain amount of time to people who are out of work).

Farm owners' income, on the other hand, depends on the size of their harvests at the end of a planting season. There is no guarantee they will make any money at all for their hard work!

What's more, saving up enough money to open even a small farm can be very difficult. Livestock, land, and equipment need to be purchased; a farmhouse and other employee living quarters need to be on the land. Unless you inherit

Farm owners typically earn higher salaries than those who just work on farms.

a farm from your parents or other family members, if you want to own a farm, you'll probably need to get some loans (money that must be paid back) from a bank or find people willing to invest (in other words, give you a certain amount of money up front in exchange for a certain portion of the farm's future profits).

"If their farm gets large enough," Angela says, "most farm owners hire agricultural managers and crop managers to supervise daily work. These farm owners are in charge of **administrative** duties such as ordering supplies for the farm; managing the different teams of farmers, ranchers, and workers; repairing and maintaining the tractors and other heavy machinery; and supervising planting and breeding decisions.

"My grandfather," Angela says, "bought our farm when he was a young man. He started out with only a few employees and had to do a lot of the daily work himself. My grandmother ran the business side of the farm—filing taxes, supervising the other employees, and selling the crops and livestock. Even when the farm started to expand and my grandmother hired more workers, my grandfather was out in the fields every day. When my father was old enough, he took over running the farm. By this time, my grandfather couldn't do as much as he used to, but even today, he is still doing chores and repairing machinery. He was never one for office work."

Angela is very similar to her grandfather. "I don't think I could ever handle any of that administrative stuff," she says. After she worked full time on the farm for a few years, Angela bought a piece of it. She still earns a salary, but now she also gets a percentage of the profits that the farm earns each year. Many farms operate this way; rather than being owned by a single person, they are owned by a family.

"When I bought into the farm," Angela says, "I could have become an administrator or even stopped working altogether. I wouldn't have had my salary, but the money that I make in profits from the farm is probably enough to support myself. But I like the work." Angela oversees the farm's livestock. She supervises a small team of people that feeds them, breeds them, and collects milk and eggs to be sold. She also handles any required veterinary work.

"We could have hired someone to take care of all this work," Angela continues, "but I don't think that I could ever give it up. It's exciting to work with animals every day. I still take our cattle out to graze, and there is nothing like a beautiful morning on the ranchland, herding a few hundred cattle through the grass. It is a part of my job that I don't think I will ever want to give up. I will probably be like my grandfather—nearly eighty years old and still waking up in the morning to feed the chickens."

SALARIES FOR FARMERS, RANCHERS, AND OTHER AGRICULTURAL MANAGERS BY U.S. STATE

Earnings for farmers, ranchers, and other agricultural managers vary by state based on demand and other factors. Here are the five states where employers pay the highest average salary and the states in which employers pay the lowest salaries.

Highest Average Salaries:	Lowest Average Salaries:
1. North Carolina: $93,780	1. Nebraska: $50,700
2. California: $92,740	2. Oklahoma: $56,970
3. Pennsylvania: $89,780	3. New Mexico: $57,480
4. Florida: $86,470	4. Missouri: $59,740
5. Kentucky: $86,310	5. Tennessee: $60,890

Source: U.S. Department of Labor

Between Angela's salary and the profits she makes as part owner of her family's farm, she usually earns around $100,000 a year. She's doing well.

AVERAGE SALARIES

"As a family farmer," Angela says, "I own part of our ranch and make a certain portion of the profits our farm makes. But how much I actually make depends on a few different things. Food prices go up and down for many different reasons. This means that the amount that agricultural buyers will pay for your crops varies all the time."

Farming can be a very risky business. For example, a severe drought devastated a large portion of the corn and soybean crops in the American Midwest a few years back. Farmers harvested very few crops. They had to raise prices on the crops they were able to produce in order to try to make enough money to keep their farms open. This kind of drought can affect the entire agriculture industry. A small harvest means that feed for livestock will also be more expensive—and when their feed is more expensive, the price of meat can go up significantly as well.

"We weren't affected too badly," Angela says, "but it was a good reminder of just how risky this business can be." Because of these kinds of risks, the U.S. government pays (subsidizes) farmers so that no matter the kind of harvest they have, they are assured to receive a certain amount of money for all their hard work.

"The government subsidies," Angela says, "can be a huge help because it is usually enough so we can pay our employees, no matter what kind of harvest we have. But it is not money that we can just keep for ourselves. When we have a really bad season, most farmers just want to make enough to keep the farm open and to not lay off any of their hands. They usually take very small salaries during these years, just enough to eat and live on, and little more than that."

Considering all the risk and added responsibility that comes with owning a farm, it is easy to understand why many farmers decide not to become farm owners. "If it wasn't for my family already owning the farm," Angela says, "I don't think I would have ever bought a farm myself. I would hate the stress of owning my own farm if I had to carry it all on my own."

Not owning a farm, however, doesn't mean that you won't still be able to make good money as a farmer. According to the USDL, agricultural managers with positions similar to that of Angela's make, on average, nearly $70,000 a year! Some agricultural managers can make as little as $35,360 a year, while 10 percent earn $135,900 or more.

Angela is luckier than most. She was born into a family and a career that she loves. She was able to purchase a piece of a farm and get both the great salary of a farm owner and the exciting work of an agricultural manager. Few people are as lucky as she is.

Most people in the United States and other developed countries live in urban and suburban areas—highly populated areas located in or close to larger towns and

A nursery worker waters plants. Greenhouse and nursery workers in the United States typically earn salaries that range from $20,000 to $33,000.

cities—where there are very few farms. The majority of young people interested in farming will have little, if any, prior experience with farmwork, and it is likely that most people in these areas do not live close enough to a farm to begin to work part time or as an apprentice in order to start to get experience. That's why most people new to agriculture will need to move to where the work is. Starting out, they won't be able to make as much money.

Eventually, many people in farming can make $60,000 a year, and you do not need a college education to make this kind of money. Most employers, however, expect a job candidate to have at least five years of experience in agricultural work before they will consider hiring them as a manager. This means working either full time or seasonally as a farmhand or agricultural worker, jobs that only pay between $20,810 and $33,270 a year, according to the USDL. However, since this is seasonal work, some agricultural workers are employed in other jobs during the rest of the year to earn more money.

You might think that the stress of moving to get a start in farming for such a small salary might not be worth it. Keep in mind, though, that most people who go to college also travel in order to get there, and they graduate, after four years, with an average $37,712 of debt, according to the *Wall Street Journal*. On the other hand, the salary of an agricultural worker or an agricultural apprentice may be small, but men and women in these positions are paid to work, learn, and get experience. An agricultural worker with an average seasonal salary of $20,000 will have already made $80,000 after four years of work (of course, you'll have bills to pay during this time) and will be only a year away from having all the experience they need to start applying to higher-paying positions. Compare that to a college graduate who enters their first job with tens of thousands of dollars of debt!

Working as a farm laborer does not pay well, but it is a good way to break into the field.

RESEARCH PROJECT

Talk to farmers who trained for the field via a technical school, apprenticeship, four-year degree program, or hands-on experience. Ask them what they liked and disliked about their training. Create a chart that shows their responses. What two types of training are the best fit for your learning style? Spend some time investigating these educational paths so that you are well prepared when it comes time to choose a training method.

TEXT-DEPENDENT QUESTIONS

1. What high school classes will be useful for those who want to become farmers?
2. What are the benefits of participating in an agricultural apprenticeship?
3. How much do farmers earn a year?

WORDS TO UNDERSTAND

arboretum: a botanic garden that is devoted to the display of trees and shrubs

botanic garden: a facility where a wide variety of plants and trees are grown and displayed for public viewing and study by plant scientists; also known as a **botanical garden**

diverse: having a lot of variety

locavore: a person who only, or primarily, eats food that is grown in their local area or region

CHAPTER 5

KEY SKILLS AND METHODS OF EXPLORATION

WHAT ALL FARMERS NEED

"Anyone in the farming business will tell you, in order to be a farmer, you have to love the lifestyle," says Angela Stevens.

A career in agriculture is challenging—and for some people, no amount of money can compensate for the long days, backbreaking physical labor, and exhaustion. Another situation a farmer faces is that most farms are located in rural parts of the country, often far away from cities or even towns. If you crave the excitement of city life, farming is definitely not for you!

But a life in agriculture also means playing a vital role in the daily life of almost every person in your country, helping to feed not only a nation but the entire world. You may not get rich or live a sophisticated city life—but the work can be fulfilling and satisfying.

"One of the best things about farming," says Chris Peterson, "is the number of different jobs available. It's hard work and not everyone will like it—but if you like working with your hands, working with animals, or operating heavy machinery, there is probably a career in agriculture you'd enjoy."

According to Chris, most people who work in agriculture are detail-oriented and work well in teams. "We need to pay attention to details," Chris says, "because one small mistake in any of the production phases can lead to a huge loss of crops at the end of the season. We also need to be able to understand weather forecasts [predictions] for the coming season to plan the best ways to plant our crops. Since the weather is always changing, so are the ways we cultivate the crops after they are planted."

Being able to be a team player is one of the ways that all details are taken into account. "There is so much that goes into farming," Chris says, "that no one person can know it all. You have to be willing to work with others to make the best decisions you can and be able to communicate these decisions to your workers and other members of the group. You can make all of the decisions that you want, but if you can't work as a team player and communicate what your group needs to do, then any decisions that you make will be useless."

Whether you are raising cattle or growing corn, most agricultural jobs require a certain amount of physical labor. You'll need to be in excellent shape because you will do a lot of walking, lifting, bending, stretching, and reaching

Farmworkers need excellent teamwork skills in order to work together to bring in the harvest. Above, farm laborers pick and box lettuce.

as you go about your work. Here are a few more key traits you'll need to be a successful farmer:

- decision-making skills
- time-management skills
- communication skills
- the ability to use technology
- the ability to lead

Farmers need a **diverse** set of skills in order to be competitive and successful. "Above all else," Chris says, "whether you decide to go to college or not, being able to learn on the job is the most important skill, especially if you want to make good money." Farm owners make the most money out of all farmers, but opening your own farm means that you need to know every bit of the process

Discover how drones are being used in agriculture.

of producing crops or livestock. The faster you can learn, the faster you'll be ready to own a farm!

EXPLORING AGRICULTURE AS A STUDENT

There are many ways to explore a career in farming. The following sections provide some suggestions.

TAKE SOME CLASSES

Hands-on learning opportunities are offered by community gardening associations, park districts, **botanic gardens**, high schools, colleges and universities, park districts, and other organizations. In these classes, you'll learn the difference between perennials and annuals, when to plant and harvest crops, and pest control techniques.

PLANT A GARDEN

One of the best ways to develop a "green thumb" is to get your hands dirty and plant, care for, and harvest your own fruits and vegetables. Some easy-to-grow fruits and vegetables include peppers, tomatoes, raspberries, strawberries, cucumbers, and beans. YouTube is an excellent source of how-to videos.

TECHNOLOGY AND FARMING

In the old days, farmers did much of their work by hand. And when they needed information about farming, they talked to the local agriculture extension agent. Today, technology has changed the way farmers do their jobs and obtain information. Here are a few of the ways farmers use technology to save time, reduce their workload, gather and assess data, and increase crop yields and animal production:

Drones are increasingly being used on farms to save time and money, as well as to improve crop yields.

- Drones are used to check on the health of crops and cattle, search for the presence of pests and flooded areas, and apply pesticides and fertilizer.
- Sensors are used to detect temperature, moisture, and other conditions to help farmers know when to plant, harvest, or perform other tasks.
- GPS technology is used in precision plowing (to ensure that furrows are aligned and not wasting farmland), in field mapping, and to improve accuracy in planting and fertilization of crops.

Planting fruits and vegetables (such as strawberries) is a great way to explore the world of agriculture.

The following books also offer good ideas:

- *Vegetable Gardening for Dummies* by the Editors of the National Gardening Association and Charlie Nardozzi
- *A Teen Guide to Eco-Gardening, Food, and Cooking* by Jen Green
- *Beginner's Illustrated Guide to Gardening: Techniques to Help You Get Started* by Katie Elzer-Peters
- *Kitchen Gardening for Beginners* by Simon Akeroyd

JOIN AN ASSOCIATION OR SCHOOL CLUB

Many countries have agricultural associations that you can join to learn more about careers in farming. For example, 4-H (https://4-h.org) is a membership organization in which you will complete hands-on projects in areas such as agriculture, health, science, and citizenship. While it is most established in the United States and Canada, 4-H reaches seven million young people in more than fifty countries. Another popular organization is the National FFA Organization (www.ffa.org), which offers career resources, competitions, and a lot of fun activities for young people in the United States. The National FFA Organization used to be called "Future Farmers of America," but it changed its name to also try to connect with people who are interested in other agriculture careers. Its members are preparing for careers in agribusiness, agrimarketing, science, communications, chemistry, education, horticulture, veterinary science, production, natural resources, forestry, and other fields.

There are similar clubs in other countries. For example, the National Federation of Young Farmers' Clubs (www.nfyfc.org.uk) provides opportunities in the United Kingdom. There are more than one hundred TeenAg Clubs (www.teenag.co.nz/clubs) in New Zealand. Junior Farmers' Association of Ontario (www.jfao.on.ca) and 4-H Canada (https://4-h-canada.ca) offer good opportunities for young people in Canada.

The National FFA Organization, 4-H, and other youth associations often work with middle schools and high schools to provide agriculture-related programs. Ask your school counselor or science teacher for information on programs at your school. If your school doesn't have an ag club, then start one!

JOIN THE SCOUTS

The Girl Scouts and Boy Scouts are membership organizations for girls and boys aged roughly five to eighteen (age ranges vary by country and group). As a member, you'll learn how to become a better person, as well as develop many new skills. When you learn something new in scouts, you usually receive a merit badge or other type of award.

The Boy Scouts of America (www.scouting.org) is open to both boys and girls. Scouts can earn a merit badge in Gardening by answering questions about nutrition, farm safety, and garden pests; visiting a botanical garden, farm, or other place where plants are grown; and building a compost bin, basic hydroponic garden, or other agricultural structure. They can also earn the following badges: Animal Science, Farm Mechanics, Plant Science, and Soil and Water Conservation.

If you're a girl, members of the Girl Scouts of the United States of America (www.girlscouts.org) can earn the following agriculture-based merit badges: Gardener, **Locavores**, and Animal Helpers.

You don't have to live in the United States to be a scout. In fact, the Boy Scouts were founded in Great Britain more than one hundred years ago. Scouting organizations in Great Britain include The Scout Association (https://scouts.org.uk) and British Boy Scouts and British Girl Scouts Association (https://bbsandbgs.org.uk). If you live in Canada, you can join Scouts Canada (www.scouts.ca). Scouts Australia (https://scouts.com.au), which was founded in 1908, has approximately 70,000 members.

TAKE A VIRTUAL FIELD TRIP

The National FFA Organization offers videos that allow you to take virtual tours in various areas of agriculture. Visit www.agexplorer.com/virtual-field-trip to view these and other virtual tours:

- The Science Behind Your Food
- Technology in Agriculture: Feeding the Growing Globe
- STEM Careers Improving Animal Health
- John Deere: Careers that Innovate

Watch as students learn more about agriculture on a field trip.

TAKE A CAREER QUIZ

If you're not sure what agricultural career you'd like to pursue, consider using the AGExplorer Career Finder (www.agexplorer.com/sites/agexplorer.com/files/career-finder). After answering thirteen questions in the categories of Education, Interests & Skills, and Career Aspirations, you'll be matched with several agricultural careers that are a good fit for your personality and career goals and interests. Further information is provided for each occupation.

ATTEND A SUMMER CAMP

Agriculture camps provide a great introduction to the environment, farming, and other outdoor-related topics. They're also great ways to meet people just like you who are interested in farming, as well as to have a lot of fun. Camps are offered by agricultural associations and organizations, local park districts, botanic gardens and **arboretums**, colleges and universities, and other providers. Here are some examples of popular camps:

- 4-H offers a variety of overnight and day camps. If you live in the United States, the best way to learn about opportunities in your area is to visit https://4-h.org/find/4-H and search for the 4-H office in your county. 4-H camps are also available in Canada and other countries.

- The U.S. Department of Agriculture offers AgDiscovery, a two- to four-week residential summer outreach program for teens who are interested in exploring careers in plant and animal science, wildlife management, agribusiness, and other fields. Students obtain experience in these fields through hands-on labs, workshops, and field trips. Learn more at www.aphis.usda.gov/aphis/ourfocus/civilrights/agdiscovery/ ct_agdiscovery_program.

- North Carolina State University's College of Agriculture and Life Sciences offers many programs for teens who are interested in agriculture and related fields, including AgDiscovery, 4-H Camps, Horticultural Science Summer Institute, Livestock Science Camp, Poultry Science Summer Institute, and VetCAMP. Learn more at https://cals.ncsu.edu/students/ my-path-to-cals/summer-programs.

CONDUCT AN INFORMATION INTERVIEW

During an information interview, you will talk to a farmer about their career. This type of interview can be conducted on the telephone, via email, or online via Skype or other videoconferencing software. Here are some questions to ask during the interview:

- Can you tell me about a day in your life on the job?
- What type of farm equipment and tools do you use?
- How has technology changed the work of farmers?
- What are the most important personal and professional qualities for farmers?
- What do you like best and least about your job?
- What is the future employment outlook for agricultural workers?
- How is agriculture changing?
- What can I do now to prepare for the field?
- If you could go back in time, would you become a farmer again?

During a job-shadowing experience, you may even get the chance to see a rancher shear a sheep.

JOB SHADOW A FARMER

During a job-shadowing experience, you observe a farmer at work. You'll watch them as they plant or harvest crops, milk cows, shear sheep, repair their tractors or combines, and perform other tasks. Be ready to get up early for your job-shadowing experience because many farmers start their workdays at 3 or 4 a.m.! While you will spend a lot of time observing, you should also ask questions during the interview. Use the list from the Conduct an Information Interview section on page 60 and 61 to get started.

Ask your school counselor or a teacher to help arrange a job-shadowing experience. Organizations such as 4-H and National FFA Organization may offer a regular schedule of job-shadowing opportunities.

SOURCES OF ADDITIONAL EXPLORATION

American Agri-Women
https://americanagriwomen.org

American Farm Bureau Federation
www.fb.org

American Society of Agronomy
www.agronomy.org

American Society of Farm Managers and Rural Appraisers
www.asfmra.org

Irish Farmers' Association
www.ifa.ie

National Farmers' Federation (Australia)
www.nff.org.au

National Farmers' Union (United Kingdom)
www.nfuonline.com

National Farmers Union (Canada)
www.nfu.ca

National FFA Organization (United States)
www.ffa.org

Visiting a farm is an excellent way to see farmers at work.

RESEARCH PROJECT

Try out three of the methods of exploration that were discussed in this chapter to learn more about agriculture and a career as a farmer. Write a two-page report that details what you learned and present it to your family and science class. Are you still curious about the work of farmers? If so, use some other strategies to expand your knowledge of agriculture.

TEXT-DEPENDENT QUESTIONS

1. Why is it important for farmers to be detail-oriented?
2. What is 4-H?
3. What are some questions that you should ask during an information interview?

WORDS TO UNDERSTAND

investors: those who are willing to contribute money to a business in the hope that they will receive a profit from their investment

middleman: a person or company that buys goods from a farmer or other producers and sells them to retailers or consumers at a higher price to earn a profit

niche: a small but profitable segment of a market

profit margin: the amount by which earnings from sales exceed the cost of running a business

CHAPTER 6

LOOKING TO THE FUTURE

OPPORTUNITIES IN AGRICULTURE

Employment for farmers and ranchers is expected to remain relatively stable between 2016 and 2026, according to the USDL. There is a trend toward larger, more efficient farms. This suggests that opportunities will be better at large farms. "Despite steady demand for agricultural products," according to the USDL, "many small farms operate with slim **profit margins** and are vulnerable to poor market conditions. As in the past, operators of smaller farms will likely continue to exit the business over the next decade."

There will be growing opportunities for farm laborers due to a shortage of seasonal workers in many countries. These jobs are not well paying and do not provide much job security. They do provide workers with an entry path into the field. In the future, some of these jobs may be replaced by automation (especially if worker shortages continue). Robot "farmers" will increasingly handle agricultural tasks such as planting, weeding, and harvesting.

Given these conditions, it's important that farmers stay optimistic, but also realistic, about the future of farming. While he hopes that the next few years will be a relatively stable period for farmers, Julián Loya, a crop manager who recently applied to a local bank for a loan to open his own farm, also says, "The future of farming is always difficult to predict. Last year's drought made us all remember that." Julián is speaking from experience. "The farm that I worked on," he says, "had a few difficult years before the drought. Difficult years happen, but you need to pick yourself up, keep working, and hope that next year will be better. After a few bad years, though, one very bad one is enough to put any farm out of business."

JOB SECURITY, ADVANCEMENT, SKILLS

For people already in the industry, stability can be a good thing. Stability in the industry means that most farmers will not have to worry about losing their jobs. Knowing you have a secure position at your place of employment and knowing that you won't be laid off for unexpected reasons is called "job security." While job security won't guarantee a raise or a promotion, it will at least guarantee a job.

For people new to agriculture or looking to advance, on the other hand, this stability will make getting jobs as agricultural managers and even agricultural workers somewhat difficult, unless you're willing to move to another area of the country where more work is available.

The most successful farmers are those who use technology to save time and money and those who are willing to embrace new farming techniques to increase crop yields.

Julián is one of those people who is willing to move in order to advance. Most people would be discouraged seeing a farm that they worked for go out of business in only a few years. Julián, on the other hand, sees it as an opportunity to advance in the industry and to do something that he has always wanted to do: open his own farm.

Julián has spent the six months after he was laid off living on his savings and taking courses at a local community college in agricultural business administration. "It is strange," Julián says. "I thought that I would learn a lot from those classes, but after so many years in the industry, I think that I already learned everything I needed to know." Julián took the classes in order to show the bank that he was prepared for everything that it takes to own and run a farm, and increase his chances of the bank approving him for a loan.

While Julián is still waiting to hear from the bank about his loan request, he isn't worried. "If the bank doesn't give me a loan, I am going to try another bank

Learn how some farmers are using automation to save money and make up for shortages of farm laborers.

and begin to seek **investors**. I know a lot about agriculture and the business of agriculture, and about being a good leader."

According to Julián, the government offers many programs to help get people involved in agricultural careers. Some of these programs offer cheap loans, while others actually give certain candidates a grant—money gifted from an organization or government in order to encourage certain industries. There are grants and loans available for a young person interested in a new career in agriculture or for people like Julián who would like to buy land to open their own farms.

GROWING AGRICULTURAL SPECIALTIES

The agricultural industry can be very competitive. Large farms—especially those owned by corporations—can often grow crops or raise animals more cost-effectively than small farms can. As a result, owners of small farms are seeking ways to develop successful market **niches** that allow them to stand out from the crowd. Some are launching organic farms that cater to people who do not want to eat crops or meat that was grown or raised with the help of harmful chemicals. Others are selling their crops directly at farmers' markets to cut out the **middleman** and earn higher profits, or raising specialty crops or animals (such as buffalo or emus) that are not offered by most farms.

Some farmers are beginning to grow cannabis, which, until recently, has been illegal in many countries. Cannabis is an annual herb that has leafy, erect stems, elongated leaves in clusters of three to seven, and pistillate flowers that spike from its branches. The term "cannabis" refers to both the marijuana

A hemp farmer checks his crops.

plant and hemp, but the two plants are different. Marijuana is increasingly being used for both medical and recreational purposes. Hemp is grown for its fiber and used to make rope, textiles, paper, and many other products. The U.S. cannabis industry alone employs 165,000 to 230,000 workers (including

DID YOU KNOW?

As of 2019, more than thirty U.S. states permitted the use of medical cannabis, and Guam, Puerto Rico, and the District of Columbia had passed similar laws. Australia, Argentina, Chile, Israel, and more than twenty European countries had legalized medical cannabis as well.

farmers). This number could more than double in the next three to five years.

IN CLOSING

Do you love growing plants or raising animals? Are you willing to work hard? Are you happiest when working outdoors? If so, a career as a farmer might be in your future. Use this book and other resources to continue to explore your interest in a career in agriculture. Do some more research. Read books and watch videos about becoming a farmer. Visit a farm to see what a typical workday is like. Plant and tend a garden to see if this occupation is a good fit for your skills and interests. Becoming a farmer is hard work and takes many hours and a lot of dedication. There are some risks to working in agriculture, but many farm and ranch owners say that they would never trade their occupation for an easier, more stable profession. Perhaps you'll say the same thing someday as you look back at your rewarding career in agriculture. Good luck with your career exploration!

Many young people are forgoing office jobs and are instead turning to careers in agriculture.

RESEARCH PROJECT

Learn more about organic farming by reading books and visiting websites about this specialty, and by visiting an organic farm. Write a 300-word report that describes the field and explains why it is becoming a popular form of farming.

TEXT-DEPENDENT QUESTIONS

1. Where will farming opportunities be stronger—at small or large farms? Why?
2. What is a grant?
3. What are some specialties that farmers are pursuing to earn more money and stay in business?

SERIES GLOSSARY OF KEY TERMS

accreditation: The process of being evaluated and approved by a governing body as providing excellent coursework, products, or services. Quality college and university educational programs are accredited.

application materials: Items, such as a cover letter, resume, and letters of recommendation, that one provides to employers when applying for a job or an internship.

apprenticeship: A formal training program that combines classroom instruction and supervised practical experience. Apprentices are paid a salary that increases as they obtain experience.

associate's degree: A degree that requires a two-year course of study after high school.

bachelor's degree: A degree that requires a four-year course of study after high school.

certificate: A credential that shows a person has completed specialized education, passed a test, and met other requirements to qualify for work in a career or industry. College certificate programs typically last six months to a year.

certification: A credential that one earns by passing a test and meeting other requirements. Certified workers have a better chance of landing a job than those who are not certified. They also often earn higher salaries than those who are not certified.

community college: A private or public two-year college that awards certificates and associates degrees.

consultant: An experienced professional who is self-employed and provides expertise about a particular subject.

cover letter: A one-page letter in which a job seeker summarizes their educational and professional background, skills, and achievements, as well as states their interest in a job.

doctoral degree: A degree that is awarded to an individual who completes two or three additional years of education after earning a master's degree. It is also known as a **doctorate**.

for-profit business: One that seeks to earn money for its owners.

fringe benefits: A payment or non-financial benefit that is given to a worker in addition to salary. These consist of cash bonuses for good work, paid vacations and sick days, and health and life insurance.

information interview: The process of interviewing a person about their career, whether in person, by phone, online, or by email.

internship: A paid or unpaid learning opportunity in which a student works at a business to obtain experience for anywhere from a few weeks to a year.

job interview: A phone, internet, or in-person meeting in which a job applicant presents their credentials to a hiring manager.

job shadowing: The process of following a worker around while they do their job, with the goal of learning more about a particular career and building one's network.

licensing: Official permission that is granted by a government agency to a person in a particular field (nursing, engineering, etc.) to practice in their profession. Licensing requirements typically involve meeting educational and experience requirements, and sometimes passing a test.

master's degree: A two-year, graduate-level degree that is earned after a student first completes a four-year bachelor's degree.

mentor: An experienced professional who provides advice to a student or inexperienced worker (mentee) regarding personal and career development.

minimum wage: The minimum amount that a worker can be paid by law.

nonprofit organization: A group that uses any profits it generates to advance its stated goals (protecting the environment, helping the homeless, etc.). It is not a corporation or other for-profit business.

professional association: An organization that is founded by a group of people who have the same career (engineers, professional hackers, scientists, etc.) or who work in the same industry (information technology, health care, etc.).

professional network: Friends, family, coworkers, former teachers, and others who can help you find a job.

recruiting firm: A company that matches job seekers with job openings.

registered apprenticeship: A program that meets standards of fairness, safety, and training established by the U.S. government or local governments.

resume: A formal summary of one's educational and work experience that is submitted to a potential employer.

salary: Money one receives for doing work.

scholarship: Money that is awarded to students to pay for college and other types of education; it does not have to be paid back.

self-employed: Working for oneself as a small business owner, rather than for a corporation or other employer. Self-employed people must generate their own income and provide their own fringe benefits (such as health insurance).

soft skills: Personal abilities that people need to develop to be successful on the job—communication, work ethic, teamwork, decision-making, positivity, time management, flexibility, problem-solving, critical thinking, conflict resolution, and other skills and traits.

technical college: A public or private college that offers two- or four-year programs in practical subjects, such as the trades, information technology, applied sciences, agriculture, and engineering.

union: An organization that seeks to gain better wages, benefits, and working conditions for its members. Also called a **labor union** or **trade union**.

work-life balance: A healthy balance of time spent on the job and time spent with family and on leisure activities.

FURTHER READING & INTERNET RESOURCES

FURTHER READING

Akeroyd, Simon. *Kitchen Gardening for Beginners: A Simple Guide to Growing Fruit and Vegetables*. London, U.K.: DK Publishing, 2013.

DK Publishing. *The Gardener's Year: Grow, Care for, and Enjoy Crops and Flowers Season by Season*. London, U.K.: DK Publishing, 2015.

Hurt, Avery Elizabeth. *Corporate Farming*. New York: Greenhaven Press, 2017.

Stone Barns Center for Food and Agriculture. *Letters to a Young Farmer: On Food, Farming, and Our Future*. Hudson, NY: Princeton Architectural Press, 2017.

INTERNET RESOURCES

www.bls.gov/ooh/management/farmers-ranchers-and-other-agricultural-managers.htm: This section of the *Occupational Outlook Handbook* features information on job duties, educational requirements, salaries, and the employment outlook for farmers, ranchers, and other agricultural managers.

www.agexplorer.com/career-interactive: This website from the National FFA and Discovery Education offers information on dozens of career paths in agriculture.

https://newfarmers.usda.gov: This website from the U.S. Department of Agriculture provides information for aspiring farmers.

www.agronomy4me.org: This website from the American Society of Agronomy offers information on the science behind growing food.

EDUCATIONAL VIDEO LINKS

Chapter 2
A young dairy farmer discusses why she loves her job:
http://x-qr.net/1HzU

Chapter 4
Learn more about agricultural apprenticeships:
http://x-qr.net/1KB9

Chapter 5
Discover how drones are being used in agriculture:
http://x-qr.net/1LSC

Watch as students learn more about agriculture on a field trip: http://x-qr.net/1Jma

Chapter 6
Learn how some farmers are using automation to save money and make up for shortages of farm laborers:
http://x-qr.net/1J6u

INDEX

most dangerous occupations in America, 24, 28
risks of owning a farm, 42–43
robot farming, 66
farmers' market, 32
farmhand
defined, 9
duties of a, 16
earnings of a, 16, 48
employment opportunities, 65–66
McBride, James, experience as a, 10–11
relocation to find work, 48, 66–67
seasonal employment, 48
training for agricultural careers, 42
farming
defined, 15
government subsidies, 46–47
high cost to start up a farm, 43–44
risks of owning a farm, 42–43, 46–47
slim profit margins, 65
specialty crops, 68–70
technology and, 55
variety of jobs available, 52
Federation of Young Farmers' Clubs, 57
fertilizer spreader, 32
fertilizers, 32
4-H clubs, 56–57, 62
Future Farmers of America (FFA), 57

G

genetically modified crop (GMC), 32
genetics
breeding livestock, 22
defined, 6, 32
need for expanded knowledge base, 10
germination, 32
Girl Scouts, 57–58
Global Positioning System (GPS), 32
greenhouse, 32

H

harrow, 32
harvesting, 21, 32
herb, 33
herbicide, 33
herbivore, 33
hydroponic gardening, 33

I

infestation, 33
insurance adjuster, 27

interviews
informational, 60–61
Loya, Julián, 66–67
McBride, James, 8–12
Peterson, Chris, 28–29, 52–53
Stevens, Angela, 42, 44–47, 51
Valencia, Christian, 16, 18–19, 21–25
irrigation system, 21, 33

J

Japanese beetles, 20
Junior Farmers' Association of Ontario, 57

L

livestock, 33
defined, 15
production of, 21–25
livestock production
breeding the animals, 22
caring for the animals, 23–24
feed for, 23–24
harvesting, 24–25
products, 21
protection from wild predators, 23
veterinary care, 24
locavore, 58
locusts, 20
Loya, Julián
future of farming, 66
seeking a loan to buy a farm, 66–67

M

manure, 33
application during cultivation of crops, 19–20
use in organic farming, 26
McBride, James
acquiring skills for agricultural careers, 8
college education, 9–10
farmhand on organic farm, 10–11
promotion to agricultural manager, 12

N

National FFA Organization, 57–58, 62
nursery, 33
nutrients, 33

O

omnivore, 33

organic farming and ranching
    components of, 25–26
    defined, 33
    goals of, 25
    manure, use of, 26
    market niche, 69
    pest management, 26
    popularity of, 25

P

parasite, 33
perennial plant, 33, 54
pest management, 33
pesticide, 21, 34
pests
    common agricultural, 20
    controlling with pesticides, 21, 54
    organic farming and ranching, 26
Peterson, Chris
    key traits of a farmer, 52–53
    lifestyle of a farmer, 28–29
pilot, agricultural, 27
plant genetics, 34
planter, 34
plow, 34
poultry, 34

R

ranch
    defined, 15–16
    ownership of, 21
rancher
    defined, 8
    duties of a, 17
    lifestyle, 28–29
    most dangerous occupations in America, 28
reaping, 34
regenerative agriculture, 34
robot, 34
robot farming, 35

S

salaries for farmers, ranchers, and agricultural managers, 45
seed drill, 35
seeding, 35
slaughterhouse, 25, 35
soil erosion, 19, 23, 35
soil nutrients, 35
sprayers, 21, 35

Stevens, Angela
    earnings of a farm owner, 42
    employees on a farm, 44–45
    government subsidies, 46–47
    lifestyle, 51
    personal income, 46
    risks of owning a farm, 46–47
stinkbugs, 20
summer camps, 59–60
sustainable agriculture, 35

T

teacher, agricultural science, 28
TeenAg Clubs, 57
threshing, 35
thrips, 20
tillage, 35
topsoil, 35
training for agricultural careers
    apprenticeships, 40–41
    four-year college, 41–42
    hands-on learning, 42
    high school, 37–38
    internships, 40–41
    vocational school, 38–39

V

Valencia, Christian
    breeding livestock, 22
    caring for the animals, 23
    cultivating crops, 19
    harvesting crops, 21
    ranch owner, 16
    slaughter of animals, 24–25
    soil erosion, 19
    three stages of crop production, 18
veterinary care, 24
viticulture, 35

W

Wall Street Journal, 11, 48
weeding, 35
whiteflies, 20

Y

yield, 35

AUTHOR BIOGRAPHIES

Andrew Morkes has been a writer and editor for more than twenty-five years. He is the author of more than twenty-five books about college planning and careers, including all of the titles in this series, many titles in the Careers in the Building Trades series, the *Vault Career Guide to Social Media*, and *They Teach That in College!?: A Resource Guide to More Than 100 Interesting College Majors*, which was selected as one of the best books of the year by the library journal *Voice of Youth Advocates*. He is also the author and publisher of "The Morkes Report: College and Career Planning Trends" blog.

Connor Syrewicz is a writer and editor from Binghamton, New York. He was raised on Long Island, has a degree in English, and spends most of his time writing and facilitating other creative projects. His interests include art and philosophy, which he actively incorporates into his writing.

PHOTO CREDITS

DATE DUE
